Tom's Mad Mop

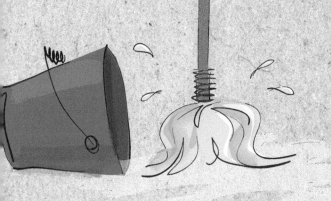

Written by Celia Warren

Illustrated by Bill Ledger

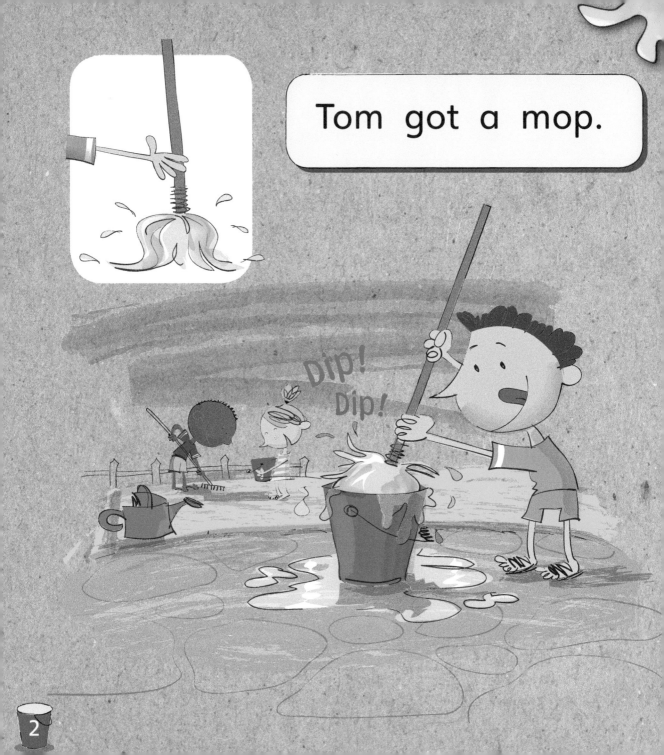

Tom got a mop.

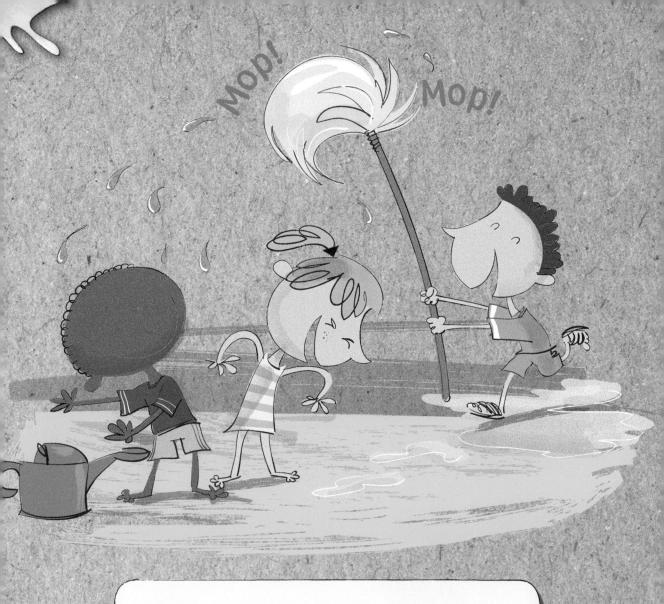

Tom's mad mop got
Kit and Mags.

3

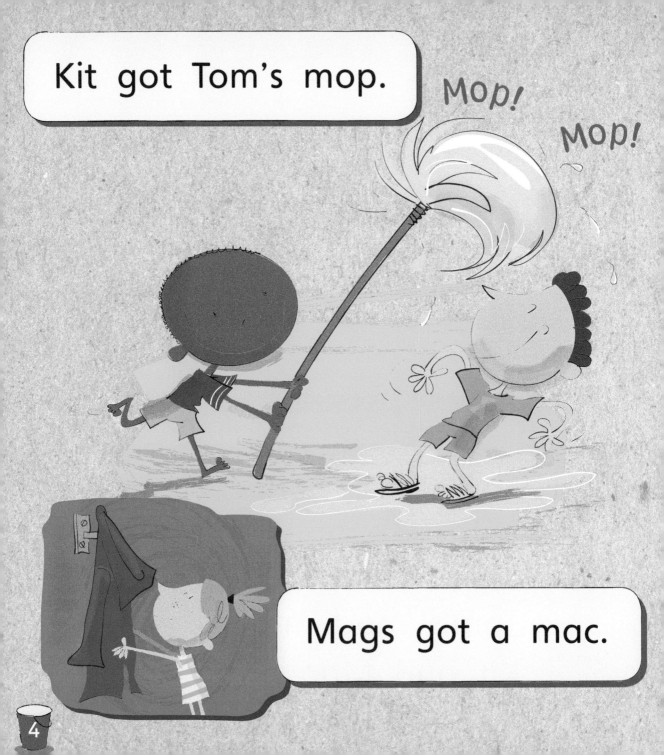

Kit got Tom's mop.

Mop!

Mop!

Mags got a mac.

4

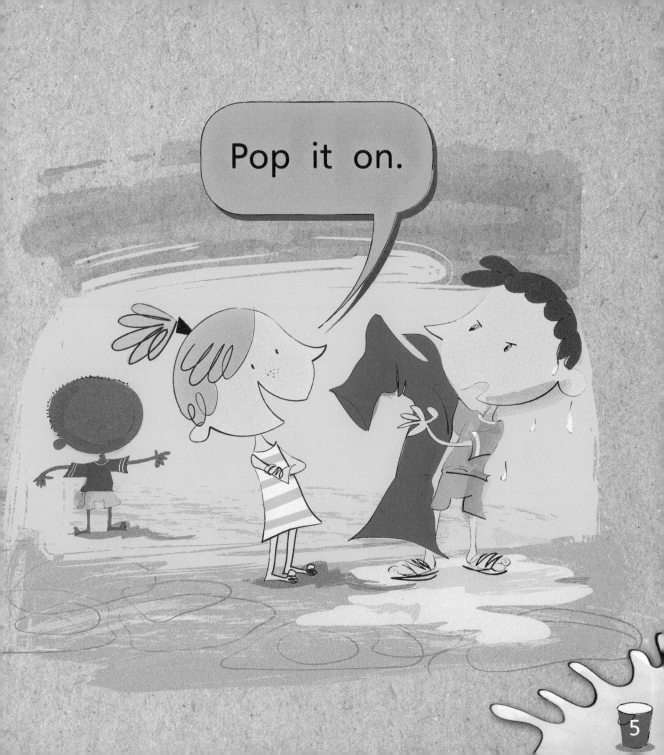

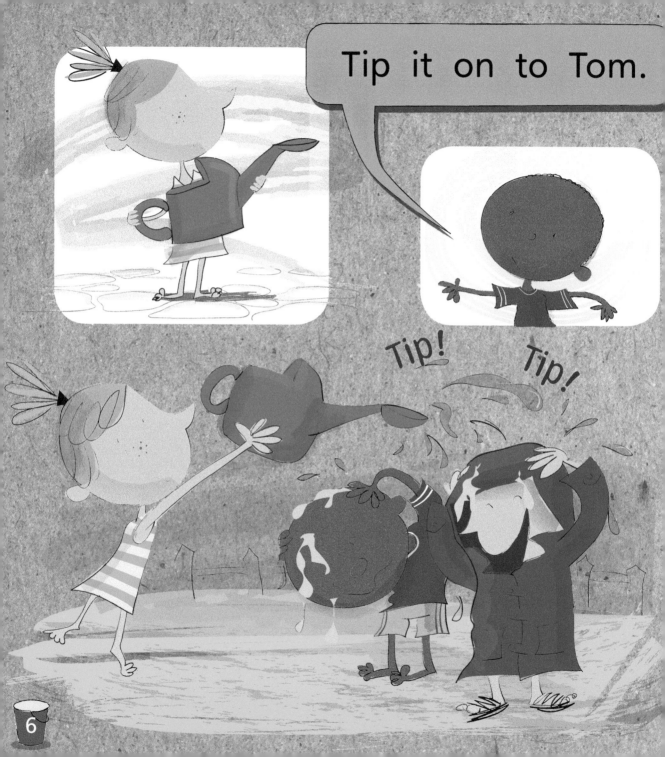

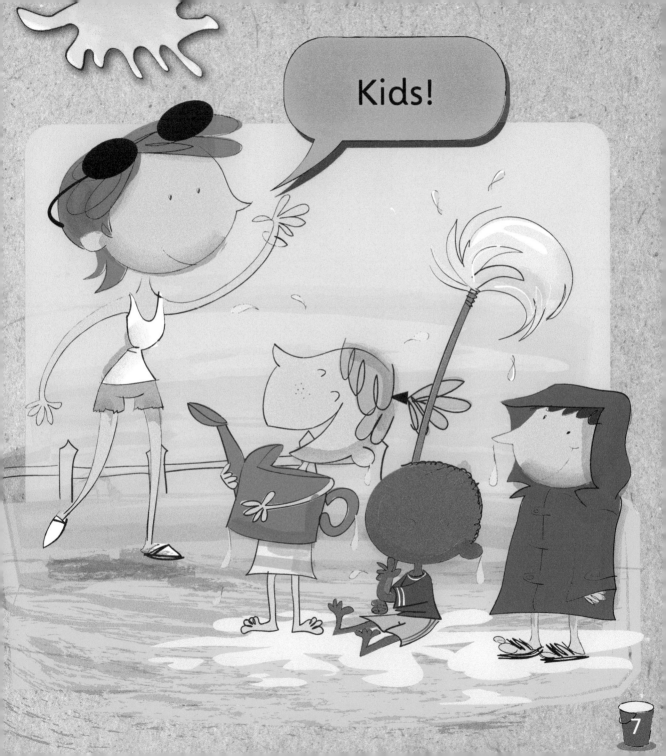

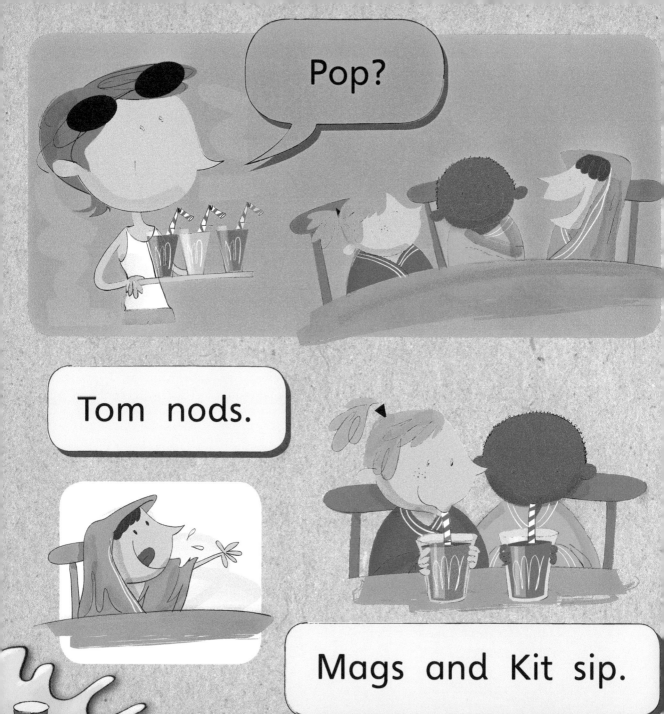

Pop?

Tom nods.

Mags and Kit sip.